Demystifying the Black Box

A Deep Dive into Explainable AI (XAI) and Machine Learning

Taylor Royce

DEDICATION

To everyone who acknowledges the responsibility that comes with technology while yet believing in its revolutionary potential. This book is dedicated to the pioneers, philosophers, and innovators who work to develop AI systems that not only push the envelope of what is possible but also serve humanity in an open, moral, and responsible manner.

To the practitioners and educators who are influencing the direction of AI, developing a new generation of accountable AI leaders, and making sure that justice and explainability are at the center of every breakthrough.

And may this book encourage you to keep challenging, learning, and enhancing the systems that are forming our world, whether you are a researcher, a policymaker, or just an inquisitive individual trying to understand the complicated world of artificial intelligence.

With appreciation for your commitment to using the potential of responsible AI to create a more equitable and open future.

DISCLAIMER

This book contains information that is solely meant to be informative and educational. Although every attempt has been taken to guarantee the content's accuracy and dependability, the author and publisher make no explicit or implicit guarantees or warranties about the content's completeness, accuracy, or suitability. The opinions and viewpoints presented in this book are those of the author and may not represent those of any institution, organization, or other body.

Professional advice in any area, including but not limited to technology, law, ethics, or business, should never be replaced by this book. For advice on particular problems pertaining to the use of explainable AI or any other subject covered in this book, readers are urged to speak with knowledgeable experts.

Any direct, indirect, incidental, or consequential damages resulting from the use or reliance on the material in this book are not the responsibility of the author or publisher. All rights reserved.

CONTENTS

ACKNOWLEDGMENTS

I want to express my sincere appreciation to everyone who helped to organize and finish this book.

First and foremost, I want to express my sincere gratitude to the leaders and specialists in the field of Explainable AI, whose labor, inventions, and research laid the groundwork for many of the concepts and ideas covered here. Your commitment to making progress in this area has been a constant source of motivation.

I sincerely appreciate the thoughts, experiences, and feedback that my peers and coworkers shared. Your insightful conversations and insightful viewpoints have influenced the focus and breadth of this work. I sincerely appreciate your encouragement and support.

I also want to express my gratitude to my friends and family for their steadfast understanding, patience, and support during the writing process. Your confidence in me kept me going, and your presence gave me the courage and insight I needed to finish this book.

Finally, I would want to express my gratitude to my readers. Your inquisitiveness, enthusiasm for learning, and dedication to ethical AI development motivate me to keep researching and exchanging concepts. I hope that this book will be a useful tool and inspire more research and development in the Explainable AI space.

This work is dedicated to everyone who believes that ethical and transparent AI can improve everyone's future.

CHAPTER 1

EXPLAINABLE AI'S ASCENT

1.1 The AI Black Box Issue

From healthcare and autonomous driving to banking and cybersecurity, artificial intelligence (AI), especially in its contemporary form through machine learning (ML) and deep learning, has revolutionized a wide range of industries. Nevertheless, despite these systems' outstanding performance, their opacity has been a recurring and expanding problem. The incapacity of humans to completely comprehend the inner workings of intricate AI models, particularly deep neural networks, is a phenomena sometimes referred to as the black box problem.

Decision-making logic is explicitly coded, traceable, and interpretable in traditional software engineering. Machine learning models, on the other hand, automatically extract patterns and representations from data, which frequently leads to complex decision boundaries and non-linear transformations that are difficult to understand intuitively. A deep neural network trained to identify cancer from medical pictures, for example, may attain 98% accuracy, but it becomes very challenging to determine why it classified one scan as benign and another as malignant. The internal layers of the model are difficult for humans to understand since they comprise dozens or millions of learnt weights.

As AI systems are used more frequently in high-stakes domains, this obscurity becomes more problematic:

- Healthcare: In order to make educated judgments, patients and physicians must comprehend the reasoning behind any diagnosis that an AI system suggests.
- Criminal justice: To guarantee equity, predictive policing or recidivism scoring systems need to be open and transparent.
- Finance: Fraud detection and algorithmic credit scoring have an influence on people's lives and need to be held accountable.

In addition to undermining trust, the black box problem makes it challenging to identify and address bias, mistakes, and unethical decision-making. Furthermore, people must have the "right to explanation" for judgments made by automated systems, according to legal regulations like the General Data Protection Regulation (GDPR) of the European Union.

Therefore, the black box aspect of contemporary AI is a fundamental obstacle to responsible, reliable, and human-aligned AI, not only a technical annoyance.

1.2 The Significance of Explainability

Explainability is essential, not optional. It is becoming more and more crucial to comprehend how and why AI systems make judgments as they continue to make significant choices in physical environments. In general, the demand for explainability can be divided into three dimensions: practical, legal, and ethical.

Moral Justifications

Biases in training data have the potential to be replicated and magnified by AI systems. For instance:

- Gender prejudice in executive posts may be unintentionally reinforced by a hiring algorithm based on previous data.
- Racial and gender differences in accuracy have been observed in facial recognition systems.

Explainability makes it possible for stakeholders to examine and contest AI judgments, spot prejudiced or discriminatory conduct, and make sure that systems adhere to moral principles of accountability, fairness, and nondiscrimination.

Adherence to Law and Regulation

As AI becomes more widely used, laws and regulations are changing to catch up. As previously stated, explainability is required by the GDPR under the principle of "meaningful information about the logic involved." In a similar vein, lenders must provide justification for credit denials under the U.S. Equal Credit Opportunity Act.

Without answers, there could be legal repercussions, harm to one's reputation, or even the ban on the use of AI systems.

Useful Advantages

The following benefits are provided by explainability from a functional perspective:

- Debugging and Model Improvement: Data scientists may detect flaws, increase accuracy, and improve algorithms by having clear insights into model decisions.
- User Trust and Adoption: When stakeholders comprehend the decision-making process, they are more inclined to embrace and depend on AI technologies.
- Collaboration and Integration: Explainability makes it possible for people to work together with AI systems in human-AI teaming settings, fostering mutual understanding.

Case Studies

1. Healthcare: IBM Watson for Oncology is a well-known example. Clinicians found the system's reasoning ambiguous and occasionally dubious, despite the fact that it was first promoted as a breakthrough in cancer therapy recommendations. Skepticism and a decline in trust in its application resulted from the lack of openness.

2. Finance: The dangers of black-box AI were brought to light by the 2019 Apple Card fiasco. Concerns regarding gender bias were raised when users reported having noticeably different credit limits. Regulatory attention was drawn to the model's incapacity to provide a coherent explanation for its judgments.

3. Legal Systems: COMPAS, an algorithm used to determine recidivism risk in U.S. courts, has come under fire for being racially biased and lacking transparency. The employment of it in court rulings has sparked a heated discussion over interpretability

and justice.

These instances demonstrate that explainability is a fundamental prerequisite for AI to operate morally and productively in society, not merely a theoretical ideal.

1.3 XAI's History and Development

The increasing complexity and opacity of contemporary AI systems has given rise to the topic of Explainable Artificial Intelligence (XAI). The formalization of XAI as a separate field of study is relatively new, despite the fact that interest in interpretable models dates back to the early days of AI.

Origins

Interpretability was not a significant issue in the early decades of AI, primarily due to the simplicity of the models themselves. Rule-based expert systems, like MYCIN (created for medical diagnosis in the 1970s), relied on explicit rules and logic that were transparent by nature. Step by step, decisions could be traced back.

Deep learning and the abundance of data, however, lead to a trade-off with AI's rebirth in the 2010s: **more predictive capability at the cost of interpretability**. The topic of "how can we make these systems explainable?" became more pressing as complicated structures such as ensemble models and neural networks gained prominence.

The Development of XAI as a Field of Study

As significant research institutes, businesses, and governments realized the need for methodical ways to analyze machine learning models, the phrase "explainable AI" started to acquire popularity in the middle of the 2010s.

The U.S. The Defense Advanced Research Projects Agency (DARPA) announcing the XAI program in 2016 was a major turning point. The objective was to create powerful and understandable learning algorithms that would help users comprehend, trust, and effectively employ AI.

Important Tools and Contributions

The XAI environment has been shaped by a number of significant tools and frameworks:

- To explain individual predictions, LIME (Local Interpretable Model-agnostic Explanations) suggests local approximations of larger models.
- SHAP (SHapley Additive exPlanations): Assigns "credit" to the features that contribute to a prediction using game theory.
- Combined Gradients and Saliency Maps: Offer quantitative or visual information on deep neural networks, especially in computer vision.

These developments contributed to the transformation of XAI from a philosophical endeavor into a tangible engineering discipline, with practitioners able to use practical tools.

Continuous Development

These days, XAI is a multidisciplinary project that includes:

- Machine Learning Research: Development of interpretable models and methods for explanation.
- Human-Computer Interaction (HCI): Creating explanations that are focused on the user.
- Ethics and Law: Matching the potential of technology with the demands of society.

Transparency is still a major concern in the area as new problems arise, such as explainability in large language models (LLMs) or generative models (like GPT or DALL·E).

1.4 Human-Centric AI, Trust, and Accountability

The foundation of trustworthy AI is explainability. Users may distrust AI systems, reject their adoption, or unintentionally abuse them if interpretability is lacking. However, concise, pertinent, and actionable explanations encourage trust, responsibility, and collaboration between people and machines.

The Multifaceted Concept of Trust

Having faith in AI entails:

- Competence: Is the system precise and dependable?
- Integrity: Are its judgments impartial and equitable?
- Transparency: Is it clear to users how it operates?
- Intentionality: Does the system behave in a manner consistent with the objectives of the user?

All of these aspects are supported by explainability. For instance, if a doctor is able to confirm that an AI system is in line with medical standards and comprehends its reasoning process, they are more inclined to trust it for diagnostic support.

Shared Responsibility and Accountability

Determining who is responsible becomes challenging when AI systems make or influence choices, particularly in legal or medical contexts. Explainability makes it possible for:

- Auditability: Detailed records of the process and rationale behind a decision.

- Controllability: AI recommendations can be rejected, modified, or intervened by human users.
- It is possible to hold designers, developers, and operators responsible for the behavior of the system.

This makes explainability a governance mechanism that guarantees the responsible usage of AI systems rather than merely a technological feature.

Systems with Humans in the Loop

Human-in-the-loop (HITL) paradigms are the direction that modern AI is heading toward, where AI enhances human decision-making instead of taking its place. In these systems:

- AI makes forecasts or recommendations.
- Humans evaluate and verify the results.
- Feedback loops make it possible to improve the system.

In this case, explainability is essential. In radiology, for instance, an AI system may identify a questionable area in an X-ray image, but a radiologist makes the ultimate diagnosis by contextually interpreting the system's data. How effectively the radiologist comprehends the AI's reasoning will determine the quality of that engagement.

Developing AI with Humans in Mind

In order to develop AI that is genuinely human-centric, explanations must be tailored to the user's cognitive needs in addition to being technically correct. This includes:

- Making technical terms easier for non-experts to understand.
- Offering exploratory interactive explanations.
- Matching explanations to the values and objectives of the user.

Building AI systems that not only produce correct results but also do so in a manner consistent with human logic, values, and expectations is the ultimate aim.

Because of the practical ramifications of implementing opaque, high-stakes decision-making systems, Explainable

AI is becoming more and more popular. Explainability becomes a fundamental tenet for creating AI that is not only potent but also morally, legally, and human-aligned as we move toward a future where machines are partners rather than tools. The following chapters will provide readers with a thorough guide to creating AI systems that genuinely make sense by delving deeper into the approaches, difficulties, and potential future directions of explainable AI.

CHAPTER 2

Artificial Intelligence Foundations

2.1 Comprehending Machine Learning and AI

The field of artificial intelligence (AI) is vast and constantly developing, encompassing a variety of methods intended to mimic human intelligence. Fundamentally, artificial intelligence (AI) is the capacity of a machine to replicate cognitive processes including language comprehension, learning, problem-solving, and perception. But artificial intelligence (AI) is a broad field with numerous subfields, such as data science, deep learning, and machine learning (ML), each with unique techniques, uses, and subtleties.

Distinguishing Data Science, AI, ML, and Deep Learning

The term "Artificial Intelligence (AI)" describes computers

or systems that mimic human intelligence. It is the broad field that encompasses any method that allows machines to replicate human actions or make choices on their own. AI can be broadly divided into two categories: general AI, which is still theoretical and seeks to reproduce the entire spectrum of human cognitive capacities, and narrow AI, which is made for certain tasks like image recognition or recommendation engines.

The creation of algorithms that enable machines to learn from data is the main goal of machine learning (ML), a branch of artificial intelligence. Machine learning models learn from data and get better over time, as opposed to being manually coded for every task. The main distinction between ML and AI is that ML is fundamentally data-driven, whereas AI may involve rules-based systems that do not learn from data.

A subset of machine learning known as "Deep Learning (DL)" uses multi-layered neural networks (hence the term "deep") to handle vast amounts of data and carry out tasks like image classification, speech recognition, and natural language processing. These networks' intricacy enables deep learning to excel at tasks involving vast volumes of unstructured input, like text and images.

In order to glean insights from data, the interdisciplinary area of data science integrates statistical techniques, data analysis, and domain-specific expertise. Data science is concerned with the entire process of gathering, cleaning, evaluating, and interpreting data in order to make informed decisions, whereas AI and ML are specialized approaches for modeling and forecasting results.

Synopsis of Reinforcement, Unsupervised, and Supervised Learning

The methods used to train AI and machine learning systems can be broadly divided into three categories: supervised, unsupervised, and reinforcement learning.

Models are trained on labeled data in supervised learning, which pairs each training sample with the appropriate output. By contrasting its predictions with the actual outcomes and modifying its parameters appropriately, the model gains knowledge. Support vector machines, decision trees, and linear regression are examples of popular supervised learning techniques. This method is applied to applications such as regression and classification.

Unsupervised Learning: Unsupervised learning makes use of unlabeled data in contrast to supervised learning. By clustering comparable data points or lowering the dimensionality of the data (e.g., Principal Component Analysis), the objective is to uncover hidden patterns or underlying structures in the data. K-means clustering and hierarchical clustering are two examples.

The process of training models by rewarding them for right actions and punishing them for wrong ones is known as reinforcement learning, or RL. By experimenting with various tactics, the model eventually learns to optimize cumulative rewards. Applications like autonomous driving, robotics, and gaming (like AlphaGo) frequently use reinforcement learning.

2.2 Trade-offs between Interpretability and Model Complexity

One of the main challenges in choosing machine learning models is striking a balance between interpretability and model complexity. More complicated models are often more accurate, but they are also more difficult to understand. When selecting the best model for a given task, it is crucial to comprehend this trade-off, especially in fields like healthcare or law where interpretability is crucial.

Simplicity vs. Complexity: Accuracy vs. Transparency

- Simple Models: Decision trees and linear regression are two examples of simple models that are frequently simpler to comprehend and analyze. The connections between input data and output predictions are clearer in these models, which contain fewer parameters. For instance, it is easy to follow the decision-making process of a decision tree, which may be displayed.

- Nevertheless, more sophisticated models might better capture the intricacies of the data than simpler models. They typically have poorer predictive accuracy, particularly when working with non-linear, high-dimensional data.

- Complex Models: Deep neural networks and other complex models may learn complex relationships in big, high-dimensional datasets. By using vast volumes of data and simulating non-linear interactions between features, these models can attain greater accuracy. For example, deep learning models are better than simple models in picture identification tasks.

- The drawback is that because of their enormous complexity, these models are usually more difficult to understand. It is almost impossible to track the model's decision-making process when there are billions of parameters and numerous layers of neurons. In important industries where knowing the reasoning behind a choice is essential, this lack of openness can be problematic.

Practical Illustrations of Model Selection Trade-Offs

- Healthcare: If interpretability is a top concern in medical diagnosis, a decision tree or logistic regression model might be better than a deep neural network. To make well-informed judgments regarding patient care, physicians must comprehend the rationale behind a model's recommendation of a specific diagnosis. Although a deep learning model may be more accurate at classifying medical images, adoption may be hampered by a lack of transparency.

- Finance: Regulators demand that algorithms in credit scoring give justifications for credit judgments. A more straightforward model, such as logistic regression, may be selected because it offers more lucid justifications for every choice, yet a more intricate ensemble model may do better in forecasting defaults. This guarantees adherence to laws such as the Fair Lending Act, which requires openness in decisions pertaining to credit.

The lack of interpretability of recidivism risk prediction tools, such as COMPAS, has drawn criticism in the criminal justice system. Despite their potential accuracy, these models' incapacity to describe the decision-making process raises concerns about accountability and justice. Even at the expense of some accuracy, it might be better in this situation to go with a simpler model that offers a more understandable explanation.

2.3 AI Model Types: Deep Neural Networks and Linear Networks

Based on their interpretability, complexity, and the kinds of data they process, AI models can be categorized. From straightforward, interpretable models to intricate, opaque deep learning networks, these are some of the most widely used models in artificial intelligence.

Synopsis of Neural Networks, SVMs, Decision Trees, and Logistic Regression

1. A decision tree is a straightforward, interpretable model that divides data into branches according to feature values in order to get a conclusion or prediction. A decision rule is represented by each

node, and a final result is represented by each leaf node. Decision trees are often used for classification problems because they are highly interpretable and simple to display.

2. Support Vector Machines (SVMs): SVMs are models for supervised learning that are utilized for problems involving regression and classification. Finding the best hyperplane to divide data classes is how SVMs operate. SVMs are nevertheless somewhat interpretable, even though they can be more complicated than decision trees, particularly in low-dimensional environments.

3. Logistic Regression: A statistical model frequently applied to binary classification issues is logistic regression. It uses a linear combination of input features to predict the likelihood of a particular class. Although logistic regression is frequently simple to understand and straightforward in its mathematical formulation, it could not work well on intricate, non-linear datasets.

4. Neural Networks: Four layers of interconnected nodes make up neural networks, especially deep learning models, which use non-linear transformations to analyze input. In high-dimensional data, these models are excellent at identifying intricate patterns. However, they are frequently hard to understand because of their intricacy. Deep neural networks are frequently employed for tasks including speech recognition, image recognition, and natural language processing.

Their Various Interpretability Levels

- Decision Trees: Very easy to understand. Decision trees are a preferred model in fields where transparency is crucial since their decisions are simple to track down.

- SVMs: Interpretable to a moderate degree. Even while SVMs provide logical justifications for their choices, it might be difficult to comprehend them in high-dimensional feature spaces.

- Logistic Regression: Very easy to understand. It is simple to comprehend the behavior of the model because the logistic regression coefficients establish a clear connection between the input data and the output prediction.

- Neural Networks: Interpretation is poor. Because deep learning models are "black-box," it can be challenging to comprehend how they arrive at a particular result. This is especially troublesome in industries like healthcare and finance where stakeholders want transparency.

2.4 Explainability and Interpretability Definitions

Two key ideas in AI are interpretability and explainability, which are sometimes used synonymously but have different meanings. Building openness, accountability, and trust in AI systems requires both.

Important Words: Fairness, Transparency, Explainability, and Interpretability

- Interpretability: The extent to which a person can comprehend the reasoning behind a machine learning model's choice. An interpretable model allows humans to comprehend how inputs are converted into outputs by offering transparent insights into its reasoning process. Compared to complicated models like deep neural networks, simple models like decision trees or linear regression are typically easier to understand.

- The capacity to give a concise, intelligible explanation of the model's decision-making process is known as "explainability." Explainability goes beyond interpretability to include actionable insights that a human can understand, whereas interpretability concentrates on the model's internal transparency. To produce post-hoc explanations for complex models, methods such as SHAP (SHapley Additive exPlanations) and LIME (Local Interpretable Model-Agnostic Explanations) may be used.

- Transparency: In AI systems, transparency is the

degree to which the model's operations are visible and available to outside examination. Stakeholders can examine transparent models, which are intended to be intelligible. This is especially important in regulated businesses where fairness and compliance depend on knowing the reasoning behind a decision.

- Ensuring that machine learning models do not discriminate against specific groups or individuals based on sensitive qualities like race, gender, or socioeconomic position is known as fairness. Since being able to describe how a model generates judgments can aid in identifying and reducing potential biases, fairness frequently interacts with interpretability and explainability.

How They Overlap and Differ

Although explainability and interpretability frequently overlap, they have distinct functions. Explainability is the process of explaining a model's logic to stakeholders who are not technical, whereas interpretability concentrates on a model's internal operations. Both are crucial in fields where it is necessary to comprehend how and why decisions are made for moral and legal reasons, such as healthcare, criminal justice, and finance.

Although the two ideas are not necessarily compatible, in practice, increasing interpretability frequently results in increased explainability. A highly interpretable decision tree, for example, may be simple to explain but may not function as well as a sophisticated deep learning model. On the other hand, even while a deep neural network may be quite accurate, it may not be very interpretable or explainable.

With a comprehensive examination of the fundamental ideas and trade-offs in the discipline, this brings Chapter 2: Foundations of Artificial Intelligence to a close. To guarantee that readers comprehend the intricacies of artificial intelligence, machine learning, model selection, and interpretability, each part has included comprehensive insights.

CHAPTER 3

EXPLAINABLE AI TECHNIQUES

3.1 International versus Local Interpretations

The idea of explanation in the context of Explainable AI (XAI) can be divided into local and global explanations. Although they have different functions and concentrate on various levels of abstraction, both are crucial for comprehending how machine learning models make decisions. It is essential to distinguish between the two methods, as well as their advantages and disadvantages, in order to completely understand these strategies.

Worldwide Justifications

The goal of a global explanation is to give a thorough grasp of how a model acts across all data points. By outlining the broad patterns, trends, and connections that the model has discovered over the complete dataset, this kind of explanation aids users in comprehending the decision-making process as a whole. Without going into specific predictions, the objective is to provide insight into the model's overall logic and behavior.

Global explanations could include, for example:

- Feature Importance: Knowing which factors, or features, have the biggest impact on the model's predictions.
- The intensity and direction of the correlations between characteristics and the target variable are shown by the coefficients in linear models, such as logistic regression.
- Decision Boundaries: Global explanations for classification problems frequently incorporate visual representations of the model's class divisions, highlighting areas of the feature space where various choices are taken.

In order to build confidence in a model, global explanations are extremely helpful, especially when it's crucial to make sure the model is acting as intended across a broad range of input data. In the case of a credit scoring model, for instance, a global explanation might show if the algorithm is consistently giving particular features (such income level) priority in a way that is consistent with the ethical standards and expectations of the domain.

Global explanations, however, could miss some of the subtleties of specific forecasts. On average, a model may perform reliably, but in certain instances, it may provide outlier predictions that the general explanation can obscure.

Local Justifications

Conversely, local explanations concentrate on elucidating specific expectations. Local explanations aim to elucidate the reasons behind a specific prediction produced for a certain input, rather than offering insight into how a model acts throughout the entire dataset. When the objective is to comprehend the reasoning behind a model's decision in a particular case, this is essential.

In fields like healthcare, finance, and criminal justice, where it's crucial to comprehend the reasoning behind a specific choice (such as whether a loan is granted or whether a patient is diagnosed with an illness), local explanations are especially helpful. In these situations, being able to describe the elements that contributed to a specific result can improve transparency and give users more confidence in the model's judgments.

The following are some examples of local explanation techniques:

- LIME (Local Interpretable Model-Agnostic Explanations): LIME trains a straightforward, interpretable model (such as a linear model) around the particular data point in issue in order to locally mimic the behavior of complex models. The forecast of that case is thus explained by the simpler model.

- SHAP (SHapley Additive exPlanations): SHAP values offer a reliable way to assign each feature's share of a model's prediction. SHAP provides a solid and statistically based explanation by calculating the average contribution of each feature to the final forecast for each case.

Local explanations provide users with the clarity they need

to evaluate specific results, whereas global explanations are useful for comprehending model behavior generally. When the stakes are high and decisions need to be understood and supported, they are invaluable.

3.2 Model-Agnostic vs Model-Specific Approaches

The two main strategies for producing explanations in the field of Explainable AI are model-specific methods and model-agnostic methods. Both strategies can shed light on how models make decisions, but they vary in how well-suited they are to particular model types and how broadly applicable they are to various algorithms.

Methods Specific to Models

Certain kinds of machine learning models are intended to be explained by model-specific techniques. These techniques are frequently closely related to the internal mechanics of the model, which increases their ability to shed light on how that specific model functions.

The following are some instances of model-specific

methods:

- Decision Trees: Decision trees are models that are naturally interpretable. A decision tree's form, in which nodes stand for options and leaves for outcomes, makes it comparatively easy to comprehend how the model makes its choices. In decision tree models, methods such as partial dependence plots can help clarify the connection between features and predictions.

- Coefficients are used in linear models (like logistic regression) to ascertain the relative contributions of each feature to the final result. The coefficients clearly show how the input variables and the anticipated results are related, and these models are naturally interpretable.

- Models Based on Rules: To create predictions, these models employ if-then principles. The decision-making process can be directly read as the rules themselves.

When working with simpler models or when a thorough understanding of a particular algorithm is needed, model-specific approaches are frequently employed. For example, where transparency is important, decision trees or linear regression models may be a desirable option for credit scoring or medical diagnosis due to their interpretability.

Model-Independent Techniques

Model-agnostic techniques do not depend on a certain model type. Rather, they are all-purpose tools that may be used with any kind of machine learning model, including neural networks, tree-based, linear, and others. These techniques either provide proxy explanations that may be read regardless of the type of model or approximate the behavior of complex models.

Several popular model-agnostic techniques are as follows:

- LIME (Local Interpretable Model-Agnostic Explanations): As previously stated, LIME fits an interpretable model (such a linear regression model) to a particular data point to produce local explanations. Because of this, it can be used to explain deep neural networks and other black-box models.

- SHapley Additive exPlanations, or SHAP: Any model can benefit from consistent feature attribution thanks to SHAP, a strong tool. Each attribute is given a relevance value according to how much it contributes to the prediction using cooperative game theory.

- The main benefit of model-agnostic approaches is their adaptability. Since they can be used with almost any machine learning model, they are a great option for elucidating intricate, opaque models such as ensemble methods and deep neural networks. However, because model-specific approaches are intended to provide explanations that are applicable to a wide range of situations, model-agnostic methods could not provide the same level of insight or precision.

3.3 Visualization and the Significance of Features

Two of the simplest and most instructive ways to describe machine learning models are feature importance and visualizations. Both methods shed light on what a model has learned, which facilitates comprehension of how particular features affect predictions.

The Value of Features

The relative contribution of each feature to the model's predictions is denoted by the term "feature importance." Feature importance in models such as random forests or decision trees is frequently calculated by assessing the relative contribution of each feature to the model's error reduction. In the decision-making process, features that are utilized often are seen as more significant than those that are used infrequently.

The following are a few ways to determine feature importance:

- Gini impurity or entropy is a metric used in decision tree-based models, such as Random Forests, to assess how well a feature splits the data at each node. Features that considerably lower entropy or impurity are valued more highly.

- Permutation Importance: This technique entails permuting a feature's values at random and tracking the degree to which the model's performance declines. Features are deemed extremely critical if they cause a significant decrease in performance when permuted.

- SHAP Values: As was previously said, SHAP values can also be utilized to assess the significance of features, offering reliable and consistent attributions in any model.

Tools for Visualization

By providing graphical depictions of how factors affect model predictions, visualization tools can further improve comprehension. Among the often used visualization methods are:

- Partial Dependence Plots (PDPs): PDPs, while keeping all other characteristics constant, illustrate the relationship between a feature and the model's anticipated result. This aids in comprehending how modifications to a certain feature impact the forecast.
- Plots that illustrate the interactions and combined effects of two or more characteristics on the model's

predictions are known as "feature interaction plots."

- Saliency Maps (for Neural Networks): Saliency maps make it easier to comprehend the reasoning behind a classification by highlighting the aspects of an image that have the most influence on the model's conclusion in image classification tasks.

When combined, feature significance approaches and visualizations offer strong instruments for revealing the inner workings of machine learning models, making the decision-making process of the model more transparent and intelligible.

3.4 Rule Extraction and Surrogate Models

Other methods to improve the interpretability of complex machine learning models include rule extraction and surrogate models. When working with black-box models, such as ensemble methods or deep neural networks, where direct interpretation is challenging, these techniques are quite helpful.

Models for Surrogacy

An interpretable model trained to approach the predictions of a more complicated, black-box model is called a surrogate model. The goal is to employ a more straightforward model that can nonetheless capture the main decision-making processes of the more sophisticated model while offering insights into its behavior.

A decision tree or linear regression model, for instance, could be used as a stand-in for a more intricate model, such as a deep neural network or random forest. An interpretable approximation of the model's decision boundaries is provided by the surrogate model, which is trained on the black-box model's outputs rather than raw data. Although they might not be able to accurately mimic the complicated model's behavior, surrogate models can provide important insights into how it makes decisions.

Extraction of Rules

The process of turning a complicated model into a collection of understandable, human-readable rules is known as "rule extraction." The objective is to reduce the decision-making process of the model to a set of "if-then" rules that are simple enough for non-experts to understand. In industries like finance, healthcare, and law, where explainability and openness are crucial, rule extraction is especially helpful.

To extract rules from complex models, decision trees are a popular rule extraction technique. Decision trees can derive basic rules that explain how a black-box model takes decisions by approximating the decision boundaries of the model.

To find hidden patterns and correlations in the data that may be turned into interpretable rules, alternative methods like association rule mining can be employed in addition to decision trees.

Practitioners can increase the interpretability of intricate machine learning models by utilizing these strategies, which will increase the AI systems' transparency and reliability. A comprehensive toolkit for comprehending and elucidating AI decisions is produced by combining global and local explanations, model-specific and model-agnostic techniques, feature importance visualizations, and surrogate models.

CHAPTER 4

HEALTHCARE DIAGNOSTICS USING XAI

4.1 The Need for Transparency in Healthcare

One of the most important industries where Explainable AI (XAI) principles need to be implemented is healthcare. Patients' lives can be drastically changed by medical diagnosis and treatment choices, therefore openness is not only desirable but also required. Clinical decision-making becomes more complex when AI is used in healthcare, but there are drawbacks as well, including issues with accountability, trust, and ethics.

Important Choices

Healthcare workers make decisions that directly affect the health and well-being of their patients. These choices, which have the potential to be life-or-death, call for accuracy as well as faith in the instruments they employ.

AI systems in healthcare often assist with activities like identifying diseases, forecasting results, and recommending therapies. But in order for these tools to be useful, they need to be clear and easy to grasp so that medical professionals can see how they come to their conclusions.

Errors cannot be held accountable without transparency. For instance, in order to repair an AI model that misdiagnoses a patient, clinicians need to know exactly why this occurred. Lack of transparency in these high-stakes situations may lead to ineffective or erroneous therapies, which could hurt patients, undermine trust, and have legal repercussions.

Safety of Patients

The top priority in healthcare is patient safety. To guarantee that patients receive the best care possible, physicians must have a thorough understanding of the thinking behind AI systems when they are used to make diagnoses or treatment decisions. Explainable AI provides a window into how these systems make decisions, enabling medical personnel to carefully examine the AI's output and confirm that it is consistent with patient history and medical understanding.

Artificial intelligence (AI) systems are especially helpful in processing large volumes of data, such genetic or medical imaging data, which may be too much for humans to handle alone. However, because of their intricacy, AI models may seem like "black boxes" to medical professionals. Clinicians could be hesitant to believe a model's advice if they don't know how it arrived at a specific diagnosis or therapy prescription. Clear explanations that shed light on the reasoning behind AI's judgments might help allay this hesitancy, increasing physician confidence and improving patient safety.

Legal Consequences

The legal ramifications of AI choices in the healthcare industry are significant. With the rising use of AI in clinical settings, healthcare companies confront the problem of ensuring that AI tools comply with regulations such as the Health Insurance Portability and Accountability Act (HIPAA) in the United States, and equivalent privacy and safety standards elsewhere. According to these rules, the diagnosis procedure and the use of private medical information must both be open and reasonable.

In order to defend its usage in a court of law, a healthcare provider must be able to explain the reasoning behind the AI's diagnosis if it is incorrect. In the absence of explainability, the healthcare professional may face legal consequences. In the event of malpractice claims or audits, XAI enables healthcare providers and organizations to prove that their AI-driven choices are supported by strong, comprehensible logic.

4.2 Case Study: Artificial Intelligence in Imaging and Radiology

One of the most well-known fields where AI is having a big influence is radiology. AI models are being used more and more to help analyze medical imaging, including CT, MRI, and X-ray scans. These artificial intelligence (AI) technologies are made to identify and diagnose diseases like tumors, fractures, and other abnormalities in pictures, frequently more quickly and precisely than human radiologists.

Explainability's Contribution to Diagnostic Trust

Explainability in AI is especially important in the high-stakes field of radiology, where a misdiagnosis can result in worse outcomes and delayed therapies. Clinicians and radiologists must have faith in the AI's judgments, but confidence can only be established when the logic underlying a model's diagnosis is transparent. Healthcare professionals would probably be skeptical of an AI system that only flags an image as having cancer without providing an explanation for its decision.

Radiologists can gain insight into how a model came to a particular conclusion by using explainable AI techniques. Explainability, for instance, can draw attention to the areas of a picture that the AI concentrated on during the decision-making process. Because of this transparency, radiologists may verify the AI's results, compare them to their own observations, and ultimately come to better conclusions.

Illustrations of Heatmaps and Visual Saliency Maps

Saliency mapping is one of the most used methods for improving the interpretability of AI in radiology. The parts of an image that most influenced the model's choice are highlighted visually in saliency maps. These maps, which indicate which areas of the original medical image the AI "found" most important in identifying a specific anomaly, can be superimposed on top of the original image.

A saliency map, for example, might draw attention to the questionable lump in a CT scan that led the AI to identify the picture as possibly having a malignancy. This enables the radiologist to confirm whether the region of the image that needs attention is in line with the AI's attention. Similar to this, heatmaps are frequently used to draw attention to areas of a picture that helped the model make a prediction. This provides a color-coded summary that is simpler to understand quickly.

In addition to increasing diagnostic confidence, these methods enable radiologists to employ AI tools as tools rather than as a substitute. Although the AI model adds another level of analysis, the healthcare practitioner still has the last say and can use the AI's justifications to confirm and cross-check the findings.

4.3 AI-Assisted Diagnosis and Clinical Decision Support

AI in healthcare is intended to support and enhance human expertise rather than replace it. Healthcare professionals can make better, more informed decisions by integrating AI into clinical operations. Transparency in these technologies is essential for building confidence and guaranteeing the best results for patients, even though AI-assisted diagnosis and clinical decision support systems (CDSS) are becoming essential tools in modern medicine.

Open AI Tools to Supplement Human Knowledge, Not Replace It

Based on patient information, including symptoms, test findings, and medical history, AI-assisted diagnosis tools can make recommendations for possible diagnosis or treatment regimens. However, these tools must be intended to be open in how they arrive at their results. Clinicians must comprehend the reasoning behind every diagnosis that an AI makes in order to evaluate its correctness.

For instance, if an AI model indicates that a patient may be at risk for a heart attack, doctors would like to know specific risk factors such as blood pressure, cholesterol, and family history the AI deemed most significant. Clinicians will be able to investigate these elements and confirm that the AI's logic is consistent with existing medical knowledge if the model is transparent.

AI can help with activities like determining medication interactions, suggesting treatments, and setting patient care priorities according to urgency in clinical decision support systems. These systems must, however, give concise justifications for their suggestions. A clinician may be able to prevent adverse outcomes by making a better decision if they are aware that a recommended prescription may interact with another medication the patient is taking.

AI-Human Cooperation in Clinical Processes

AI should be viewed as a cooperative partner that improves

physicians' capacity for prompt and accurate decision-making, not as a substitute for them. AI-powered solutions, for instance, may swiftly examine enormous datasets, find trends, and offer insights that may not be immediately obvious to the human eye. To evaluate the findings, make thoughtful choices, and guarantee that patient care is still personalized and compassionate, human skill is still required.

The delivery of healthcare can be greatly enhanced by human-AI collaboration in clinical workflows, especially when doctors are overloaded with data. AI can enable physicians to use data more effectively and efficiently by giving them comprehensible explanations, which will ultimately improve patient outcomes.

4.4 Handling Fairness and Bias in Medical AI

AI models are commonly trained on enormous datasets, but if these datasets contain biases, the AI systems will reflect and perpetuate such prejudices. Biases in AI in healthcare can have major repercussions, such as disparate treatment for certain demographic groups. An AI model that was predominantly trained on data from one ethnic group, for instance, would not work well for patients from other ethnic groups, which could result in incorrect diagnoses or less-than-ideal care.

How Systemic Biases Are Revealed and Corrected by Explainable AI

The capacity of explainable AI to reveal and draw attention to biases in AI models is one of its main benefits. It is simpler to identify which features or attributes are influencing the model's judgments when explainability approaches like feature significance and saliency mapping are used. It is possible to detect and address biases in models that place an excessive emphasis on characteristics like socioeconomic class, gender, or race.

For example, even in cases when race shouldn't be a determining factor, it may be discovered that a healthcare AI system disproportionately prioritizes race when forecasting specific diseases. Healthcare practitioners can investigate how these biases affect judgments and take remedial action to lessen them when AI is transparent. This is particularly crucial to guaranteeing that AI systems are just and equal, offering all patients, regardless of their background, the same caliber of care.

Ensuring Medical AI Systems Are Fair

Identifying and resolving biases is simply one aspect of addressing fairness in medical AI; another is making sure the model is trained on representative, diverse data. This can lessen the possibility that decisions will be influenced by systemic biases. Additionally, healthcare practitioners can use explainable AI to make sure that the model's predictions are founded on reasonable and pertinent criteria.

Healthcare professionals may guarantee that AI systems are not only accurate but also morally and impartially sound by employing strategies that encourage openness. This will guarantee that patients receive fair treatment regardless of their demographic traits.

By increasing transparency, boosting clinician trust, encouraging human-AI collaboration, and addressing bias and fairness, XAI plays a critical role in healthcare diagnostics. Explainability will be crucial as AI develops in the medical domain to guarantee that these instruments are reliable, accurate, and morally sound. Explainable AI can be included into healthcare systems to assist medical personnel in making more educated decisions, which will eventually improve patient care and results.

CHAPTER 5

LEGAL, ETHICAL, AND REGULATORY ASPECTS

It is crucial to navigate the regulatory, ethical, and legal landscape with a thorough understanding of the frameworks that govern these innovations as AI technologies, particularly Explainable AI (XAI) , become more and more integrated into vital industries like healthcare, finance, and law enforcement. Many concerns of responsibility, equity, and the rights of those impacted by AI systems are brought up by their implementation. The different legal frameworks, moral precepts, and risk management techniques that surround the creation and application of AI systems particularly with regard to explainability will be examined in this chapter.

5.1 Legal Frameworks and the Right to Explanation

A idea that comes up in legal conversations about AI use, especially when it comes to decision-making processes that have an impact on people's lives, is the right to explanation. The emergence of AI systems in fields including criminal justice, healthcare, credit scoring, and recruiting has raised awareness of this idea. Legal frameworks are being established in a number of nations and jurisdictions to guarantee that people are aware of the process by which automated decisions are produced and have the ability to contest decisions that they believe to be unfair.

Emerging AI Governance, GDPR, and HIPAA

The General Data Protection Regulation (GDPR) has emerged as a key piece of legislation in the European Union when it comes to protecting people's rights in an AI-driven environment. A particular clause in the GDPR known as the "right to explanation" grants people the right to know how automated decisions that have a big impact on them are made. According to this rule, people must be given relevant information about the reasoning behind automated processing, including how their data is being used and any possible repercussions.

- GDPR: Article 22 of the GDPR expressly addresses automated decision-making, including profiling, and stipulates that unless specified requirements are fulfilled, people should not be subjected to decisions that are made exclusively using automated processing. A human review of the automated judgment is necessary if the AI system has a substantial influence on an individual (as in the case of employment or credit scoring choices). Furthermore, every AI-generated result's decision-making process may be explained upon request by the data subject.

- HIPAA (Health Insurance Portability and Accountability Act) in the United States requires the protection of patient data in the healthcare industry, but it also subtly addresses the need for openness when medical judgments are made by AI systems. The growing use of AI for diagnosis and treatment recommendation raises concerns over the interpretability of these systems, even though HIPAA primarily addresses data security, privacy, and access rights. According to HIPAA, patients are entitled to see their medical records and learn how they are being utilized, including whether artificial intelligence is being employed in their treatment.

Other regulatory frameworks are appearing globally as AI develops further. To create a legal framework for AI governance, for instance, the European Commission has put up new AI legislation that emphasizes risk management, responsibility, and transparency. These rules contain clauses requiring AI developers to justify their conclusions, especially when such decisions have a significant influence on people's lives.

Consequences for Institutions and Developers

It is crucial for AI engineers to comprehend and abide by legal frameworks such as GDPR and HIPAA. Because of these standards' demands for accountability and openness, developers must consider explainability while designing their systems. Organizations that use AI systems need to make sure that they can be audited and that they can give comprehensible justifications for the decisions they make automatically.

- In their AI models, developers must incorporate explainability mechanisms like decision trees, feature importance rankings, and visual explanations like saliency maps and heatmaps.
- Institutions must set up explicit procedures for informing people about AI-driven judgments. This may entail creating a specialized staff to manage requests for data access and disseminate details about the algorithms that underlie these decisions.

The organization or business adopting AI systems may face severe fines, legal issues, and reputational harm if these legal frameworks are broken. Therefore, it is essential to create AI systems that are both technically sound and adhere to changing legal requirements.

5.2 Principles of Ethical AI Design

As AI technologies advance and become more widely used, there is a growing emphasis on making sure AI systems are developed and used in an ethical manner. The FAT principles fairness, accountability, and transparency are the most prominent of the fundamental ideas that underpin ethical AI design. These guidelines direct the creation of AI systems that uphold social norms and human rights.

Equity

Since biased algorithms can provide unfair results, especially in fields like recruiting, lending, law enforcement, and healthcare, fairness is a crucial factor to take into account while developing AI systems. AI systems must be made to treat everyone equally, making sure that no group is unjustly disadvantaged because of their socioeconomic background, gender, age, or race.

Developers must make sure that their training data is representative of the entire population and diverse in order to attain fairness. When AI models are trained on non-representative datasets, biases frequently infiltrate the algorithms, leading to distorted predictions that reinforce inequality. Regularly auditing and testing models to identify and fix any biases that might have developed during training is one way to address fairness in AI.

Responsibility

The goal of accountability is to hold AI system developers and implementers accountable for their deeds and the results of their models. If an AI system makes a choice that hurts a person or a community, there needs to be a clear way to hold those accountable. This covers the organizations that use the AI system as well as the developers that create it.

AI systems need to be auditable and explicable in order to enforce accountability. It should be feasible to track down the decision-making process and pinpoint the error's location if an AI commits a mistake. Better governance and regulatory monitoring of AI systems are made possible by this transparency, guaranteeing that they function within the moral bounds set by society.

Openness

An essential component of ethical AI is transparency. Customers, workers, and patients alike can all gain insight into the decision-making process through transparent AI systems. In addition to increasing confidence in AI systems, transparency makes it possible to spot possible issues or biases before they have a negative effect.

By employing tools and strategies like model interpretability methods, which let users comprehend how models function and the reasoning behind their decisions, developers can increase transparency in AI. Making these models interpretable facilitates auditing and reviewing AI systems to make sure they are operating as intended and in accordance with ethical standards.

5.3 Liability and Risk Management in AI Systems

Although AI systems are made to make decisions based on data, there should be explicit rules for assigning blame in the event of an error, such as a biased employment decision or an inaccurate medical diagnosis. This section examines how AI systems handle responsibility and risk management.

Assigning Accountability When AI Misleads or Fails

Assigning blame becomes challenging when AI systems malfunction or generate false results. Because AI systems, particularly deep learning models, are so complicated, even their designers could not fully comprehend how the system came to a given result. The issue of culpability becomes much more urgent as a result.

The engineers who built the system, the organizations that implemented it, and the people who maintained or altered it are frequently held accountable in the event of an AI failure. However, since many AI systems are meant to learn and adapt over time, figuring out liability can be difficult.

Developers and institutions must make sure they have strong systems in place for monitoring AI decisions and results in order to manage these dangers. This may entail putting in place logging systems that document the inputs, operations, and results of AI models. These logs offer a transparent record of how decisions were made and who is accountable when something goes wrong.

Risk Mitigation Through Monitoring and Audits

Regular audits and ongoing monitoring are two of the best strategies to reduce the dangers related to AI. Periodically assessing AI systems is necessary to make sure they continue to operate morally and correctly. AI system monitoring enables early error or anomaly detection and quick intervention before damage is done.

An AI system used in healthcare, for instance, should undergo routine audits to make sure it continues to provide correct diagnoses and is not introducing biases. Similar to this, AI systems used in hiring or credit scoring should undergo routine testing to make sure they are not unintentionally discriminating against particular groups.

5.4 XAI Deployment Standards and Guidelines

Standards and guidelines are being developed as AI continues to advance to assist enterprises in implementing AI systems in a way that is morally righteous, open, and consistent with the law. A number of organizations have created guidelines and best practices that can direct the creation and implementation of explainable AI systems.

Guidelines and Best Practices for the Industry from Groups Like IEEE and ISO

Guidelines and standards that support the development of responsible AI have been released by the International Organization for Standardization (ISO) and the Institute of Electrical and Electronics Engineers (IEEE). The main goal of these frameworks is to guarantee that AI systems are made to be open, equitable, responsible, and safe.

- IEEE: A set of guidelines on ethically aligned design for intelligent and autonomous systems has been released by the IEEE. These principles support the use of XAI to make AI systems easier to comprehend and manage, as well as the inclusion of ethical issues in the AI design process.
- ISO: In order to guarantee that AI systems are reliable and consistent with society norms, ISO has also released guidelines on AI governance. When deploying AI technologies, these standards assist firms in adopting best practices, especially in vital

industries like healthcare, finance, and law enforcement.

Developers and organizations may make sure that their AI systems are constructed with accountability and transparency in mind by following these rules. These guidelines also offer a framework for making sure AI systems are used sensibly and in accordance with the law and ethical standards.

There are many different and constantly changing legal, ethical, and regulatory issues pertaining to AI and explainable AI. To guarantee that AI systems are developed, implemented, and controlled in a way that upholds people's rights and guarantees justice, accountability, and transparency, developers, organizations, and legislators must collaborate. We can guarantee that AI technologies are applied ethically and successfully for the good of society by abiding by regulatory frameworks like GDPR and HIPAA, adopting ethical AI design principles, controlling risks, and adhering to industry standards.

CHAPTER 6

XAI FRAMEWORKS AND TOOLS

The emergence of Explainable AI (XAI) has significantly changed the way that machine learning models are thought of, created, and applied. Although artificial intelligence (AI) systems, especially deep learning models, have shown impressive potential, questions of accountability and transparency have been raised by their complexity and the "black-box" nature of their decision-making processes. Understanding and elucidating AI systems' decision-making processes is crucial since they are used more and more in industries like healthcare, finance, and law. This chapter will examine some frameworks and technologies that make it possible to create machine learning models that are both interpretable and explicable. These tools are intended to help developers, end users, and regulatory agencies better comprehend complicated models so that the results of these systems can be relied upon and verified.

6.1 LIME: Interpretable Local Explanations Independent of Models

In the XAI field, one of the most popular tools is LIME (Local Interpretable Model-Agnostic Explanations). Its main objective is to explain machine learning models that are normally challenging to understand, particularly when it comes to black-box models like deep neural networks. In order to approximate the behavior of complicated models for individual predictions, LIME builds local surrogate models. This makes it possible to comprehend the model's decision-making process on an individual level, even in cases when the underlying model is intricate.

How LIME Works and When to Use It

In order to produce new synthetic instances that are somewhat different from the original data but still similar, LIME disturbs the data instances it is attempting to explain. A straightforward, interpretable model (such a decision tree or linear regression) that mimics the behavior of the more complex model in the local region of interest is then trained using these perturbed instances.

- Step 1: Perturbation: By making minor adjustments to the characteristics, LIME creates variations of the input instance at random. These disturbed data values are subsequently supplied into the black-box model.
- Step 2: Training a Surrogate Model: Using the altered data points, a straightforward, interpretable model (such as a decision tree) is trained to approximate the behavior of the black-box model in that immediate neighborhood.
- Step 3: Explanation: The black-box model's conclusion for the specified instance is explained using the surrogate model.

Because LIME is model-agnostic, it may be used with almost any machine learning model, including support vector machines, random forests, and deep neural networks. It is especially helpful when the objective is to comprehend individual forecasts and provide explanations for the reasons behind a model's particular choice in a given situation.

Advantages and Drawbacks

Advantages:

- Interpretability: LIME offers interpretable, local explanations that shed light on a model's decision-making process for certain cases.
- Flexibility: It can be used with a variety of machine learning models because it is model-agnostic.
- Ease of Use: LIME requires little modification to current machine learning workflows and is comparatively simple to deploy.

Limitations:

- Local Explanations: LIME only explains specific forecasts, not the general behavior of the model. As a result, it might not reveal information about the model's overall behavior or patterns of decision-making.
- Instability: The complexity of the surrogate model and the selection of perturbations may have an impact on the explanations' quality.
- It can be computationally costly to generate altered

examples and train a surrogate model for every explanation, especially when dealing with big datasets.

6.2 SHAP: Additive explanations for SHapley

Another effective method that uses feature significance values to explain the output of machine learning models is called SHAP (SHapley Additive exPlanations). The foundation of SHAP is Shapley values, a cooperative game theory idea that fairly rates each feature in a machine learning model according to how it affects the final prediction.

A Game-Theoretic Method for Attributing Features

The concept of a fair payout distribution in a cooperative game, where participants (features) work together to accomplish a goal (prediction), is the source of Shapley values. A feature's average contribution to every possible combination of characteristics used to create a forecast is represented by its Shapley value. Each feature's Shapley value is determined by SHAP, which offers a local and global explanation of how features affect the model's predictions.

By taking into account every conceivable feature combination that could have been utilized in the model, SHAP determines the contribution of each feature for a given prediction. The weighted average of a feature's marginal contributions over all potential feature combinations is its Shapley value.

Comparing LIME

Although machine learning models are explained by both LIME and SHAP, their methods are very different:

- Local vs. Global: LIME gives local explanations by approximating the model's behavior for specific predictions. SHAP, on the other hand, can offer both local and global explanations, shedding light on the significance of traits generally as well as how they affect particular forecasts.
- Model-Agnostic vs. Model-Specific: LIME is model-agnostic, meaning it may be applied to any

machine learning model. Though it can be used with other models, SHAP is made to function well with a range of models, including tree-based techniques like random forests and gradient boosting machines.

- Because SHAP is based on Shapley values, which have strong mathematical underpinnings, it offers explanations that are more accurate and theoretically supported. Although helpful, LIME's explanations might not be as trustworthy, particularly in cases when surrogate models are unstable.

SHAP's Advantages and Drawbacks

Advantages:

- Theoretical Foundation: SHAP's feature importance values are fair and consistent since it is based on cooperative game theory.
- Global and Local Interpretability: SHAP offers both local explanations (information about specific predictions) and global explanations (information about the behavior of the entire model).
- Consistent Feature Attribution: Even for various model types, SHAP values offer dependable and

consistent attribution of feature relevance.

Restrictions:

- Computational Complexity: Shapley value calculations can be computationally costly, especially for models with a lot of features, which makes them impractical for huge datasets.

- Limited Flexibility: SHAP may not be as adaptable or simple to use as LIME in some situations, particularly when dealing with extremely complicated models, even though it performs well for many models.

6.3 Other Open-Source Libraries, Captum, and InterpretML

A number of open-source tools have surfaced to assist developers in implementing interpretable models as the need for explainable AI increases. These libraries make it simpler to incorporate interpretability into AI processes by offering pre-built tools and algorithms for producing explanations of machine learning models.

Essential Python Packages for Creating Interpretable Theories

- InterpretML: InterpretML is a sophisticated library that supports both global and local interpretability approaches for machine learning models. Decision trees, linear models, and black-box models like deep neural networks are just a few of the many techniques it supports. The library provides several interpretability approaches such as Partial Dependence Plots (PDP), Individual Conditional Expectation (ICE) plots, and Explanatory Models (EM).

- Use cases: InterpretML is particularly helpful in developing interpretable models when working with high-dimensional and complicated datasets, which makes it appropriate for sectors such as healthcare and finance.

- Captum: Facebook created the PyTorch-based library Captum, which offers a collection of neural network interpretability methods. It supports methods that are very helpful for comprehending deep learning models, such as Integrated Gradients, Saliency Maps, and Layer Attribution.

- Use cases: Captum is ideal for deep learning applications, particularly in fields where neural networks are frequently employed, such as computer vision and natural language processing.

- Alibi is an additional open-source toolkit for machine learning interpretability that provides both model-specific and model-agnostic explanation tools. Alibi is compatible with techniques such as Feature Importance, Counterfactual Explanations, and Anchor (for rule-based explanations).

- Use cases: Alibi is perfect for scenarios where you need to give developers and end users thorough, intelligible explanations of machine learning models.

Integration Advice and Use Cases

- Use Cases: These libraries are especially helpful in

fields like healthcare, finance, and law where transparency and trust are crucial. For instance, a financial organization may use InterpretML to make sure that its credit scoring models are transparent and equitable, or a healthcare provider may use Captum to describe how a deep learning model arrived at a diagnosis.

- Integration Tips: Take into account the computing resources available when incorporating these tools into your workflow, since many interpretability methods can be computationally costly. It's also critical to modify your explanation strategies to meet the unique requirements of your audience and model. For instance, you may utilize LIME to provide local explanations for specific forecasts or SHAP to gain a global understanding of a model's behavior.

6.4 Constructing Unique XAI Pipelines

Creating a custom XAI pipeline entails creating a methodical plan for integrating interpretable machine learning models into your project or company. This procedure entails picking the right frameworks and tools, incorporating them into current processes, and making sure that the explanations are precise and useful.

A Comprehensive Approach to Developing Interpretable Systems

1. Define the Scope of Interpretability: Identify the audience (e.g., data scientists vs. end-users) and the degree of interpretability required (e.g., local vs. global explanations).
2. Select the Right Tools: Depending on the model type, interpretability needs, and computational resources, pick the proper XAI frameworks (e.g., LIME, SHAP, Captum).
3. Integrate with Machine Learning Models: Make sure that explanations are produced in addition to model predictions by integrating the chosen XAI tools into your current machine learning pipelines.
4. Evaluate the Explanations: Determine how well the XAI tools produced the explanations. Are they precise, useful, and consistent with the real

decision-making process of the model?

5. Refinement and Optimization: Keep improving the XAI pipeline to increase computational efficiency and explanation quality.

Best Practices for Scalability and Maintainability

- Modular Design: Create reusable, modular parts that are simple to update or replace when new interpretability techniques are developed.

- Automation: Create explanations for model predictions automatically, making it a component of the standard pipeline for model deployment.

- To make sure the explanations stay accurate as the model changes over time, test and validate their efficacy on a regular basis.

Organizations may build scalable, maintainable XAI systems that offer transparency and confidence in their AI models by adhering to these best practices.

The frameworks and tools for explainable AI are always changing and provide a variety of effective approaches to increasing the transparency of machine learning systems. These technologies are crucial for improving the understandability and reliability of AI systems, whether via LIME, SHAP, or specific libraries like InterpretML and Captum. Developers can create AI systems that not only make accurate predictions but also offer concise, useful insights into the process by which those predictions are generated by skillfully utilizing these technologies.

CHAPTER 7

DIFFICULTIES WITH XAI IMPLEMENTATION

Transparency and interpretability are crucial in the new era of machine learning and AI systems brought about by the emergence of Explainable Artificial Intelligence (XAI). The decision-making processes of AI models must be understood by both the creators and the end users who depend on their outputs as they get increasingly complicated and are incorporated into high-stakes industries like healthcare, banking, and law. Nevertheless, there are many obstacles in the way of attaining effective explainability. These difficulties stem from the necessity to provide explanations that are understandable to non-experts, the inherent trade-offs between interpretability and model complexity, and the requirement to customize explanations for various stakeholders. Significant challenges are also presented by the technological difficulties of scaling XAI systems in practical applications.

The accuracy-interpretability dilemma, user comprehension and cognitive biases, the difficulty of explaining to different stakeholders, and the technical challenges of scalability and performance are some of the most significant obstacles to XAI implementation that we will examine in this chapter. These concerns are essential to comprehending the difficulties involved in creating transparent, reliable AI systems and guaranteeing their successful implementation.

7.1 The Dilemma of Accuracy and Interpretability

The accuracy-interpretability dilemma is at the center of many XAI issues. The trade-off between a machine learning model's explainability and predictive power is known as this problem. Deep neural networks and other extremely precise models are frequently the hardest to interpret. These multi-layered models are excellent at producing accurate forecasts, but they offer little to no explanation of how they are arrived at. On the other hand, less complicated models, such decision trees or linear regressions, are easier to understand but may not be as accurate for complicated tasks.

Managing Trade-offs Without Performance Compromise

In fields where high accuracy and clear explanations are equally important, the problem is particularly noticeable. In the medical field, for instance, a deep learning model may be used to identify illnesses from medical images; yet, because of the model's intricacy, it may be practically impossible to comprehend how it arrived at a specific diagnosis. A more transparent model, on the other hand, might be simpler to comprehend but might not reach the same degree of diagnostic precision.

Methods for dealing with this problem consist of:

- Model Agnostic Approaches: Using model-agnostic methods to explain complex model outputs, such as LIME or SHAP. Despite their potential to shed light on black-box models, these tools have drawbacks in terms of the amount of explanation they can offer and the computational burden they entail.

- Interpretable Machine Learning Models: Scientists are trying to create new models that are accurate and interpretable. Although they are still in the research stage and have not yet gained widespread use, interpretable neural networks and other techniques that balance complexity and transparency are beginning to take shape.

- Hybrid Models: Combining intricate, precise models with more straightforward, understandable models is an additional strategy. To create a hybrid system that strikes a compromise between accuracy and interpretability, a model might, for example, utilize a deep learning architecture for prediction and a decision tree or rule-based system for explanations.

- Post-Hoc Explanations: Saliency maps and attention mechanisms are examples of post-hoc explanation techniques that can be used to highlight the features that had the greatest influence on the decision-making process, even when employing complex models. This approach offers a measure of interpretability without compromising accuracy.

In the end, resolving the accuracy-interpretability conundrum necessitates a thorough comprehension of the relevant use case and a readiness to accept compromises in accordance with the demands of the particular application.

7.2 Cognitive bias and user comprehension

Even when explainable AI models are created, there is no guarantee that their explanations will be comprehensible. Technical specialists and regular consumers are among the users of AI systems, and it can be difficult to communicate complicated model decisions in a way that non-experts can understand. Furthermore, even if these explanations are technically valid, users' interpretations may be influenced by cognitive biases.

Making Non-Experts Understand Explanations

Explanations of AI forecasts must be adapted to the end-user's cognitive capacities and background information in order to be understood. For example, a data scientist might benefit from a very technical explanation, while a business executive or doctor might find it too much to handle. Therefore, identifying the audience and developing explanations appropriately is a crucial stage in developing XAI systems.

A few tactics to enhance user comprehension are as follows:

- Simplification without Oversimplification: While explanations ought to be succinct and straightforward, they must avoid oversimplifying the logic of the model. A system's credibility may be damaged by misleading interpretations that result from oversimplification. For instance, giving a single, extremely basic explanation for a complex deep learning model's decision-making process (e.g., "the model is confident because it saw a large amount of data") could give the user a false sense of understanding and mislead them about the actual nature of the decision-making process.

- Visual Explanations: Data visualization appeals to

humans by nature. Visual aids such as decision trees, saliency maps, and feature significance plots can help non-experts understand difficult decisions. Users are better able to understand the reasoning behind decisions when clear graphics are used.

- Narrative Explanations: Sometimes it works especially well to give explanations in the form of a story. An explanation of an AI model's reasoning can aid in bridging the knowledge gap between users and intricate model mechanics. A medical diagnosis model's choice, for instance, might be made more approachable by breaking it down into a step-by-step reasoning process, much like a clinician could.

Dangers of Exaggerated or False Interpretations

Although understanding requires simplification, there is a thin line separating simplification from misleading explanations. The explanation may leave out important information or subtleties that could cause misinterpretation if it oversimplifies the decision-making process. A model that identifies people as high-risk for a particular disease, for instance, might just use one factor such as age to explain the classification. The final choice, however, may take into account a number of intricate variables, such as genetic information, lifestyle choices, and medical history. Users may place undue weight on a single element if the explanation is overly simplified, which could skew their perception of the model's decision-making process.

7.3 Providing Clarification to Various Stakeholders

Explainability is made more difficult by the variety of stakeholders who engage with AI systems. When it comes to comprehending how AI models operate, different groups such as data scientists, clinicians, regulators, and end-users have different needs. To ensure openness and build confidence in AI systems, explanations must be customized to these stakeholders' demands.

Customizing Justifications for Clinicians, Regulators, and Data Scientists

The technical proficiency of each stakeholder group varies, as do their demands for the explanations they need:

- The most technically skilled stakeholders are usually data scientists, who are able to comprehend intricate explanations incorporating statistical metrics, activation functions, and model weights. They might favor in-depth, quantitative information that can assist them in debugging the model or comprehending its behavior in greater detail. Giving them Shapley values or model coefficients, for instance, could be a useful method of explaining the behavior of the model.

- Clinicians: In fields such as healthcare, clinicians could require explanations that are both understandable and pertinent to medicine. Since they are usually not data scientists, they might not be familiar with complicated algorithms or technical language. However, since these choices may have an immediate impact on patient care, they require justifications that are enough to foster confidence in the AI's suggestions. In this case, rule-based systems, decision trees, or simplified models that provide a clinical explanation of AI reasoning are helpful.

- Regulators: To make sure AI models are being used morally and in accordance with the law, regulatory agencies want clear and intelligible explanations of them. Fairness, accountability, and openness should be the main topics of explanations for regulators. This can entail sharing details about the data the model uses, how it was trained, and how it guarantees non-discrimination.

- End-Users: Explanations must be straightforward and practical for regular users. In a financial model, for instance, a customer will find it more meaningful to explain a loan refusal in terms of affordability or credit history rather than delving deeply into the inner workings of the model.

It takes flexibility and adaptation to create explanations that satisfy the interests of various stakeholders. One of the most important steps in making sure the AI system is trustworthy and understandable is to customize explanations for particular audiences.

7.4 Bottlenecks in Scalability and Performance

Lastly, it is crucial to take into account the scalability and performance of XAI systems in practical applications, even though the significance of explainability cannot be emphasized enough. In many AI deployments, the computational overhead associated with producing explanations particularly for huge datasets or extremely complicated models can be a major bottleneck.

Technical Challenges in Explainable System Scale Deployment

It can be costly and time-consuming to generate explanations for every forecast or choice a model makes in large-scale systems. For example, SHAP computes Shapley values for each feature, which can be computationally demanding, whereas LIME necessitates creating numerous perturbed copies of an input.

- Latency Issues: Low-latency decision-making is essential in many real-time applications, such financial transactions or autonomous driving. The AI system's usefulness may be compromised if producing an explanation takes too lengthy, particularly in situations involving frequent or real-time decision-making.

- Resource Constraints: Using computationally demanding XAI techniques can strain resource-constrained environments. It might not be possible to generate explanations in scenarios with limited computational resources (such as embedded systems or mobile devices).

Methods and Solutions for Overcoming Scalability Issues

Several tactics can be used to lessen performance and scalability bottlenecks:

- Approximation Techniques: Approximation techniques that strike a balance between speed and accuracy can be employed in place of precise explanation calculations. For instance, there may be a fair trade-off between interpretability and performance when estimating the behavior of complicated models using surrogate models such as decision trees.

- Efficient Algorithms: To lessen the computing load, researchers are creating more effective XAI algorithms. As an illustration, SHAP has created TreeSHAP, which significantly reduces the time and processing resources needed by optimizing the Shapley value calculation for tree-based models.

- Edge Computing: Edge computing can be utilized to transfer the computational load of explanation generation to adjacent servers for applications in resource-constrained contexts. This lowers latency and guarantees that decisions made in real-time can still be explained.

There are many obstacles to overcome when implementing explainable AI, including the trade-off between accuracy and interpretability, the difficulty of guaranteeing user comprehension, customizing explanations for various stakeholders, and overcoming scalability.

These difficulties show that designing AI systems requires a well-rounded, interdisciplinary approach that preserves the model's performance integrity while prioritizing openness, equity, and technical viability.

CHAPTER 8

DESIGNING WITH HUMANS IN MIND IN XAI

Explainable AI (XAI) has become increasingly important as artificial intelligence (AI) continues to infiltrate many industries. Users need AI systems they can comprehend and have faith in, in addition to having faith in the systems they engage with. In order to achieve this, the idea of Human-Centered Design (HCD) in XAI has become a guiding philosophy. By emphasizing the user's wants, preferences, and constraints, human-centered design puts them at the center of the development process. This entails developing XAI systems that provide clarity, trust, and relevance in their justifications.

This chapter explores the importance of human-centered design in XAI, highlighting the relevance of feedback loops and interactive explanations, the importance of co-creation with domain experts, and how it promotes trust and transparency. We will also look at how to assess the value of explanations using relevant metrics and user research.

8.1 Creating Transparency and Trust in Design

Developing user trust is one of the core issues in the XAI space. Trust is crucial, especially in fields like healthcare, banking, and law where the AI system is making judgments that have an immediate effect on people's lives. Transparency and clarity in explanations must be given top priority by developers in order to create AI systems that promote trust.

Principles of UX/UI Design for AI Interfaces

In order to make AI explanations understandable and practical, user experience (UX) and user interface (UI) design are essential components. The cognitive burden of users, their comprehension of complicated information, and their expectations from the system must all be taken into account by the design principles that guide UX/UI for AI interfaces. Among the crucial design tenets are:

- Simplicity and Clarity: Without overburdening consumers with technical jargon, explanations should be brief and straightforward. For example, in a financial application, an AI system might highlight important details like income, credit score, and loan amount in clear language to explain why a loan application was denied. A non-technical person should be able to understand the explanation without delving into computational specifics.

- Consistency: Information presentation should be consistent across the design. In order to foster familiarity and lessen cognitive overload, users should anticipate seeing comparable explanation forms and terminologies across various AI system applications.

- Visual Aids: Charts, heatmaps, and graphs are examples of visual aids that can make it easier for people to understand explanations. Heatmaps, for instance, can be used by a healthcare AI model that forecasts disease outcomes to identify the regions of a medical image that were most important in making the diagnosis. These visual aids make it easier for consumers to understand how the model makes decisions.

- User-Friendly Interactions: AI explanations should be accessible to users through interface design. This entails including interactive elements like hover-over tooltips, clickable explanations, or even chat interfaces where users may ask follow-up questions regarding the model's choices.

How User Trust Is Affected by Explanations

How much users trust an AI system is largely determined by its explanations. Users are frequently left wondering about the system's fairness, dependability, and the rationale behind its decisions when AI models function as "black boxes." Clear and intelligible answers can greatly increase confidence by:

- Demystifying the Model's Behavior: Users can better comprehend the logic behind AI predictions when clear explanations are provided. Users are more inclined to trust an AI system and its results when they understand the reasoning behind a particular decision.

- Reducing Anxiety and Resistance: AI choices can induce dread and anxiety in high-stakes applications such as law enforcement or healthcare. Giving customers concise, intelligible explanations can ease their anxiety by convincing them that the system is impartial, transparent, and equitable.

- Encouraging User Engagement: Users are more inclined to interact with and confidently use AI systems when they comprehend how the algorithms arrive at their decisions. A trustworthy system promotes pleasant user experiences, and trust is the cornerstone of long-term user relationships.

- Encouraging Accountability: Explicit explanations encourage accountability, particularly when making decisions that affect people's lives. Users should believe that they have enough information at their disposal to question or support the system's judgments, whether they are related to a loan denial or a medical diagnostic.

8.2 Interactive Feedback Loops and Explanations

Giving a static explanation is insufficient, even though giving precise explanations is crucial. Additionally, an efficient XAI system should provide feedback loops and enable interactive explanations. In addition to expanding the user's comprehension, this dynamic interaction between the user and the system encourages control and participation in the decision-making process.

Resources That Let Users Ask "Why" or "What If"

A strong layer of interactivity is added by giving users the option to query the AI model and request more explanations or investigate alternative scenarios. The following are some methods and resources that make this easier:

- Why Explanations: Users could be interested in knowing how the model came to a specific conclusion. For instance, a user of a self-driving automobile system could wish to know why the vehicle chose to stop or slow down. The system can offer comprehensive insights into the factors that impacted the selection, such as traffic, pedestrian activity, and road conditions, by letting users inquire "why" the choice was chosen.

- Users' comprehension of how various inputs impact the model's outputs can be substantially improved by interactive tools that allow them to investigate "what if" scenarios. By changing different criteria, including income or debt level, users could observe how their credit score changed and learn more about the reasons influencing the system's decisions.

- AI systems have the ability to include real-time feedback loops, in which the behavior of the AI is influenced in real-time by the actions or inputs of users. In a medical diagnosis system, for example, a physician might modify specific inputs, such as symptoms or medical history, and immediately observe how the model's advice changes. Users feel empowered and in control of the decision-making process because of this interactive element.

Building Interaction to Increase Trust

By making the model's decision-making process transparent, interaction increases trust. Users are more likely to have faith in the system's dependability and equity if they are able to investigate alternative inputs or pose follow-up queries. Additionally, this interaction can assist in pinpointing potential weak points or biases in the model, which can subsequently be fixed through ongoing development.

8.3 Collaborating with Subject Matter Experts

Including domain experts in the development process, or co-creation, is a crucial component of human-centered design in XAI. These professionals offer insightful information on the particulars and context of the field in which the AI system will be used. Developers can make sure the model and its explanations are pertinent, helpful, and in line with the demands of users in the field by working with domain experts.

Using Users to Help Create Interpretable Models

Although end users should be able to understand AI systems, users, especially subject matter experts, should actively participate in the design process. These professionals are frequently most suited to determine which characteristics and inputs are most important for comprehending AI choices. Including them in the process of developing the model guarantees that the explanations are both technically solid and relevant to the context.

In the medical field, for instance, physicians and clinicians might offer advice on the most crucial components of a diagnosis or prescription as well as the best way to communicate them. Developers can use this information to create systems that explain the model's choices in a way that is consistent with healthcare providers' professional expertise.

Involved Design in Finance, Healthcare, and Other Fields

In many industries, including healthcare, finance, and education, participatory design has been shown to be a successful approach. The difficulties and subtleties that AI models must handle are frequently well understood by domain specialists in these fields. The resulting system is more likely to generate explanations that cater to the individual needs of users when these specialists work with developers.

Participatory design in healthcare can guarantee that AI systems provide diagnosis and treatment recommendations in a manner consistent with best practices and medical protocols. It assists in making sure that risk assessments, loan approvals, and fraud detection systems in finance provide precise and understandable justifications that regulators and customers can rely on.

AI systems are more likely to produce insightful, pertinent, and intelligible explanations that appeal to users and stakeholders when domain experts are included in the design process.

8.4 Assessing the Utility of Justifications

The ability of XAI systems to produce explanations technically alone is not enough to determine their efficacy; they also need to be evaluated in terms of how effectively those explanations meet user needs. It is crucial to assess the usefulness of explanations in order to improve XAI systems and make sure they live up to user expectations.

Metrics and User Research to Evaluate the Quality of Explanations

Developers must employ both qualitative user research and quantitative measures to evaluate the quality of AI explanations. Typical methods for assessing the quality of an explanation include:

- A good explanation should accurately depict the model's decision-making process and offer a thorough analysis of all the variables that affected the choice. It is essential to assess whether an explanation is error-free and covers all pertinent topics.

- Understandability: The user's ability to understand the explanation is one of the most important KPIs. User studies can be used to evaluate this, asking people to score how understandable and clear the explanations are.

- User Satisfaction and Trust: After users engage with the explanations, surveys and feedback forms can be utilized to determine how satisfied they are with the system. A key determinant of the explanation's utility is trust. Users are more inclined to accept the AI's judgments if they believe in its logic.

- Task Performance: In certain situations, the effectiveness of an explanation can be assessed by looking at how successfully users complete tasks after getting it. In a medical AI system, for example, doctors may be asked to choose a course of therapy based on the AI's suggestions. It is an indication that the explanations are helpful if they enable them to make more precise decisions.

By means of these assessments, developers can consistently enhance the quality of explanations, guaranteeing that they are not simply precise but also genuinely beneficial for users.

Human-centered design in XAI highlights the importance of clear, intelligible, and user-focused explanations. We can develop AI systems that are not only technically sound but also in line with user requirements and expectations by working with domain experts, integrating feedback loops and interactive explanations, designing for trust, and evaluating the usefulness of explanations. This strategy guarantees that AI technologies are more reliable, inclusive, and useful in practical applications.

CHAPTER 9

EXPLAINABLE AI's FUTURE DIRECTIONS

In recent years, explainable AI (XAI) has advanced significantly, giving trust and transparency to AI systems in a range of industries, including healthcare and finance. But there are still a lot of obstacles to overcome and AI is still in the early stages of development. The demand for more complex, nuanced explainability strategies is growing as the profession expands. The future directions of explainable AI are examined in this chapter, with particular attention paid to the following important new fields: causal explainability, the function of generative AI and large language models (LLMs), real-time explainability for edge and IoT devices, and XAI for multimodal AI systems. In addition to being at the forefront of XAI research, these fields also reflect the potential and real-world problems that will influence AI in the years to come.

9.1 In the Direction of Causal Explainability

Understanding causality is one of the biggest problems facing AI today. Without necessarily comprehending the underlying causal links, the majority of machine learning models, particularly those used in deep learning, rely on correlation to find patterns and associations between data sets. Despite their potential strength, correlation-based models frequently fail to offer explanations that accurately reflect the rationale underlying their predictions.

Transitioning to Causality-Aware Models from Correlation-Based Models

The need for explanations that go beyond simple correlations is increasing as AI is incorporated more and more into high-stakes fields like healthcare, autonomous driving, and legal decision-making. By enabling AI systems to recognize and elucidate the cause-and-effect links that inform their judgments, Causal explainability seeks to close this gap. Causality provides considerably deeper insights by revealing why an event or choice occurs, in contrast to correlation, which just displays patterns.

Instead of merely saying, for example, that "high blood pressure correlates with heart disease," a causal model would describe how high blood pressure causes particular alterations in the cardiovascular system, which in turn results in heart disease. This type of explanation is much more actionable since it gives consumers the knowledge they need to make wise decisions or take preventative action.

A number of intriguing methods are being investigated to introduce causality into AI, such as:

- With the use of these methods, artificial intelligence (AI) systems can now simulate causal linkages as opposed to merely associations. Techniques such as Granger causality and do-calculus are designed to assist machines in identifying and measuring causal linkages.

- The probabilistic models known as "Causal Bayesian

Networks" illustrate the causal links between variables and offer a framework for understanding how modifications to one variable may affect other variables.

- The "what if" scenarios are the main subject of counterfactual explanations. "What would have happened if the input had been different?" is one of the queries it responds to. This offers a better understanding of how the model makes decisions and can assist in determining the underlying causes of particular forecasts.

- We may develop AI systems that not only make predictions but also provide an understandable and useful explanation of their thinking by shifting toward causal models.

9.2 Explainability in Big Language Models and Generative AI

By producing text, visuals, and even code that resembles that of a person, generative AI and large language models

(LLMs), as GPT-3, have transformed natural language processing (NLP) and other fields. But in spite of their extraordinary powers, these models are frequently referred to as "black boxes." Models such as GPT are notoriously hard to grasp due to their size and complexity. Generative models deal with unstructured data and use deep, complicated structures that lack simple explanatory frameworks, in contrast to typical AI systems, which frequently rely on structured data and relatively simple feature engineering.

Difficulties in Understanding Transformer-Based Models, Such as GPT

Large volumes of data are used by generative models, especially transformer-based architectures, to discover complex linguistic patterns, however these models do not always provide explicit explanations for their results. This makes it extremely difficult to comprehend why a specific text or response was produced. Important difficulties include:

- Transformers like GPT work by processing a lot of

text via a number of hidden layers, where the judgments made at each layer are not readily accessible or understandable. This is known as the "opacity of internal mechanisms." It's still difficult to understand why the model produced a given sequence or selected particular terms.

- Vast Scale and Complexity: Models such as GPT are so large (with billions of parameters) that it is challenging to comprehend how the model generates a given result. Saliency mapping and feature significance are two examples of traditional model interpretability techniques that have trouble offering practical insights into such huge, high-dimensional models.

- Generative models are sensitive to the input text and frequently produce responses based on context that may not be immediately obvious to a user. This is known as contextual ambiguity. Because of this, it might be difficult to explain why a particular response was produced, particularly in open-ended circumstances where models yield surprising results.

Attempts to Make Generative AI More Explainable

Despite these obstacles, a number of strategies are being investigated to increase generative models' explainability:

- Attention Mechanism Visualization: Transformers mostly use attention processes to identify the most pertinent portions of the input text. Researchers can learn more about the model's focus areas when producing replies by displaying attention weights. This can provide some hints as to which aspects of the input influenced the outcome, even though it does not completely explain the reasoning process.

- In order to provide post-hoc explanations for transformer-based models, methods such as LIME (Local Interpretable Model-Agnostic Explanations) and SHAP (SHapley Additive exPlanations) are being modified. By altering inputs and monitoring the ensuing changes in outputs, these methods provide a local approximation of the model's behavior and offer a better understanding of the factors influencing the model's predictions.

- The following are counterfactual explanations and input perturbations: Input perturbation techniques, in which the model is given slightly modified versions of the original input and the consequences on the output are examined, can be used to better understand model behavior. Understanding the circumstances in which the model would produce a different outcome can also be aided by counterfactual reasoning, in which users ask, "What if the input were different?"

- We can get closer to a day when even intricate models like GPT can be comprehended, relied upon, and consistently applied in crucial applications by increasing the transparency of these generative systems.

9.3 Explainability in Real Time for Edge and IoT Devices

As artificial intelligence (AI) spreads, it is being used more and more in edge computing and Internet of Things (IoT) settings where processing speed and efficiency are crucial. These settings frequently function with severe resource constraints, including constrained memory, bandwidth, and processing power. This presents a special problem for explainability: how can AI systems deliver precise, useful explanations in real time without sacrificing accuracy or performance?

Modifying Justifications for Low-Latency, Restricted Settings

The requirement for real-time decision-making in edge and IoT environments necessitates that AI models function well while producing quick forecasts. Conventional explainability techniques, like intricate feature significance scores or intricate visualizations, might be too resource-intensive or slow for these kinds of settings. Whether it's a smart thermostat that modifies the temperature of the room according to user behavior or a smart security camera that examines video to identify possible dangers, the necessity for clear and intelligible decisions is equally important in these situations.

A number of tactics are being developed to address these issues:

- Model compression, which minimizes the size of AI models without significantly compromising speed, is one of the main techniques for attaining real-time explainability in edge AI. It is possible to simplify models while preserving a degree of interpretability that can be effectively implemented on low-powered devices by using Pruning, quantization, and distillation.

- Local Explanations: Edge AI systems are able to produce local explanations as an alternative to depending on intricate global models that demand a lot of computation. These explanations use streamlined logic that is simpler to calculate in real-time and center on a particular choice or forecast. For example, a smart sensor may use a few important input features to justify a choice to signal an anomaly.

- Streaming Explanations: streaming explanations may become crucial in dynamic contexts such as the Internet of Things, where data is continuously generated. As new information becomes available, these justifications can be produced instantly, offering real-time insights into the decision-making process. For instance, depending on the incoming flow of traffic data, a smart traffic light system may produce an explanation for the reason it changed from green to red.

- Edge-Based Model Training and Explainability: In certain situations, edge devices may carry out some local model training and explanation creation instead of sending data to the cloud for processing. This guarantees quicker reaction times and lessens the need for continuous contact with centralized servers.

- Explainable AI can proliferate in practical applications by creating effective, real-time explanations that make AI systems more reliable and usable even in limited settings.

9.4 Multimodal AI Systems and XAI

Explainability faces additional issues with the emergence of multimodal AI systems that incorporate many types of data, including text, images, audio, and video. Although these systems are frequently more robust and adaptable than single-modal models, it becomes far more difficult to explain their choices. Complex explainability frameworks that can manage the complexities of integrating data from several sources are necessary in multimodal systems to comprehend how various modalities interact to inform a choice.

Illustrative Models that Integrate Text, Pictures, Sound, and More

Various forms of data are used in multimodal AI systems to inform overall decisions. For instance, in order to detect a problem in a medical imaging system, an AI model may examine X-ray images in addition to patient history (text data). It is important to think carefully about how each modality affects the ultimate choice and how to effectively convey these influences to consumers in order to explain such systems.

A number of strategies are being investigated to address these issues:

- Cross-modal attention mechanisms assist models in concentrating on the most pertinent elements of every modality when choosing one. It may be easier to understand which elements of a written document or image had the greatest influence on the model's prediction if these attention weights are visualized.

- Unified Explanation Models: Some strategies seek to provide a single, coherent explanation that integrates data from all input kinds by unifying explanations across modalities. To ensure that the final explanation is correct and understandable, this calls for complex reasoning and integration procedures.

- Post-hoc Multimodal Explanations: To deal with multimodal AI, researchers are developing techniques like LIME and SHAP, which are similar to the usage of post-hoc explanations in single-modal systems. These techniques assist users comprehend the contribution of each data source by approximating the ways in which the various modalities influence distinct aspects of the model's decision.

• The creation of interpretable frameworks that may provide a uniform, transparent explanation of these intricate models will be crucial to the broad acceptance of multimodal AI systems as they continue to improve.

Addressing these various issues and enhancing the capabilities of existing methods are key to the future of explainable AI. Researchers and practitioners can advance the development of more transparent, reliable AI systems by concentrating on causal explanations, generative models, real-time limitations in edge and IoT contexts, and multimodal systems. These developments will guarantee that AI models not only function well but also provide users with insights that are relevant, actionable, and intelligible, ultimately leading to increased acceptance and trust in AI technologies.

CHAPTER 10

THE PATH AHEAD: ESTABLISHING CONSCIENTIOUS AI ENVIRONMENTS

The need for responsible AI ecosystems has never been greater as AI permeates every aspect of our lives, from healthcare and education to entertainment and transportation. To ensure that AI serves mankind in a way that is not just effective and creative but also transparent, responsible, and in line with societal norms, it is imperative that ethical practices and explainable AI (XAI) be incorporated into AI development and deployment. The future of responsible AI is explored in this chapter, with a focus on important areas where big progress can be made. These include education for the next generation of AI practitioners, real-world case studies and success stories, empowering users with AI insights, and building a culture of explainability within institutions and organizations.

10.1 Training the Upcoming AI Professionals

Making sure that the upcoming generation of AI practitioners is prepared to comprehend, create, and apply AI technologies in an ethical, transparent, and explicable way is one of the most essential components of creating responsible AI ecosystems. The first step in doing this is incorporating the ideas of explainable AI (XAI) and AI ethics into professional development courses and academic curricula.

Including Ethics and XAI in Academic Programs

Giving students the abilities and information required to handle the challenges of AI development must be a top priority for educational institutions as AI continues to influence sectors and communities. AI's ethical ramifications and the requirement for transparency should be highlighted in addition to its technological features, such as machine learning algorithms and neural networks.

- Curriculum Reformation: Courses on data privacy, bias detection, ethical issues with AI, and the effects of AI systems on society must be incorporated into traditional computer science and AI curricula. The cornerstone of AI education should include the ideas of justice, openness, responsibility, and inclusivity.

- Coursework Specific to XAI: In addition to ethics, explainable AI should be the focus of specialized courses. These would teach students how to create models that are not only accurate but also interpretable by going over the theory, methods, and applications of XAI. Additionally, they must be instructed on how to strike a balance between explainability and model performance, particularly in intricate settings like natural language processing and deep learning.

- Interdisciplinary Collaboration: Technical know-how is not enough to drive AI advancement. Educational programs can promote a more comprehensive knowledge of the implications of AI systems by encouraging cooperation between AI technologists and experts in the fields of law, sociology, psychology, and philosophy. Students will be able to approach ethical problems from a variety of perspectives thanks to this interdisciplinary approach, which will guarantee that the AI systems they develop fairly serve a range of populations.

Continuing Education for Present Practitioners

Continuing education is essential for current AI practitioners to stay up to date with ethical standards and technological breakthroughs. By providing XAI and AI ethics certificates, workshops, and seminars, practitioners will be equipped to develop and use AI in an ethical manner. This training for professionals should concentrate on:

- Explainability must be incorporated into AI models.
- How to explain and explain AI choices to stakeholders who are not technically inclined.
- The best methods for detecting and reducing bias in artificial intelligence systems.
- Legal and regulatory issues pertaining to accountability and transparency in AI.

We can guarantee that the AI workforce maintains its competence, responsibility, and accountability in the face of swift technological developments by cultivating a culture of learning and ethical reflection.

10.2 Success Stories and Industry Case Studies

Looking at real-world examples where explainability and transparency have had a quantifiable impact can help demonstrate the revolutionary potential of XAI. Companies and organizations are starting to implement ethical AI practices across a variety of sectors, including healthcare, banking, and law enforcement, showcasing how XAI can enhance decision-making, foster trust, and reduce risks.

Healthcare: Using XAI to Improve Decision Support

AI has the ability to completely transform patient care in the healthcare industry by producing more precise diagnosis and treatment regimens. However, both patients and medical experts are concerned about the opacity of AI decision-making, especially in life-or-death scenarios. By guaranteeing that the logic underlying AI-driven medical decisions is clear and intelligible, XAI provides a solution to this problem.

- IBM Watson for Oncology Case Study: Explainability features enable medical professionals comprehend how IBM Watson's AI system, which helps oncologists diagnose and prescribe treatments for cancer patients, came up with its recommendations. Watson gives clinicians the ability to make well-informed decisions based on the model's insights by offering not just the diagnosis but also the supporting information, logic, and possible alternatives. Better patient outcomes result from increased trust between physicians and patients brought about by this degree of openness.

Case Study:

- Breast Cancer Detection System by Google Health: Google Health created an AI algorithm that can accurately identify breast cancer in mammograms. In order to give clinicians confidence in the system, the model was created with an understandable interface that revealed which aspects of the mammography were most important in making the diagnosis. This openness facilitates radiologists' comprehension of the model's logic, which makes it simpler to validate or modify the diagnosis as needed.

These case studies show how XAI can improve AI's efficacy and credibility in crucial industries like healthcare, where comprehension and actionability are crucial.

Finance: Using Explainable Risk Models to Establish Trust

AI is utilized in the financial sector to evaluate creditworthiness, forecast market trends, and identify fraudulent conduct. AI-driven financial decision-making's lack of transparency, however, has the potential to erode confidence and create legal issues. By offering concise, intelligible justifications of decision-making processes, XAI can reduce these risks, which is essential for both compliance and customer confidence.

- Zest AI Case Study: Machine learning algorithms are used by Zest AI, a business that specializes in

AI-powered credit assessment, to evaluate credit risk. The company has included explainability into its models to enhance consumer trust and guarantee adherence to fair lending standards. Through a clear explanation of the variables affecting a credit score, Zest's platform enables borrowers to comprehend the reasoning behind their credit decisions. In addition to assisting with regulatory compliance, this gives customers the ability to take remedial action if necessary.

Law Enforcement: Making Sure Predictive Policing Is Fair

In order to anticipate criminal activities and distribute resources, AI has also been utilized in predictive policing. However, calls for greater accountability and transparency in AI systems employed in law enforcement have arisen due to worries about prejudice and impartiality. By offering explanations of how AI algorithms generate predictions, XAI can allay these worries and guarantee that choices are made in a fair and equitable manner.

- PredPol Case Study: Law enforcement organizations employ PredPol, a predictive policing program, to anticipate crime hotspots. But its opacity has sparked questions about fairness and racial bias. Making the data inputs and forecasts more transparent has been the main goal of efforts to incorporate explainability into PredPol's decision-making process. PredPol's transparency can be increased to assist ensure more equitable and responsible use by disclosing how the model makes predictions based on past crime data and enabling police departments to evaluate and modify the system.

These case studies demonstrate the significant influence that XAI can have on enhancing accountability, transparency, and justice in sectors where decision-making and trust are essential.

10.3 From Openness to Self-determination

Explainable AI's ultimate objective is to enable users whether they be customers, financial advisers, or healthcare professionals to take action based on the insights that AI systems provide, rather than merely making AI judgments transparent. Users must be able to comprehend the rationale behind AI's judgments and utilize this knowledge to make well-informed decisions; transparency alone is insufficient.

Taking Action Instead of Just Understanding

AI systems must be created with the end user in mind, offering not only understandable but also useful explanations. In order to enable users to **act** on the insights AI offers, it is necessary to give them explanations that enable them to use the data in realistic, useful situations.

Case Study:

- Legal Assistants Driven by AI: Artificial intelligence (AI) tools are utilized in the legal sector to examine case files and find pertinent precedents. These systems frequently offer justifications for the relevance of a certain precedent. The explanations could be expanded to include practical suggestions, including possible methods for constructing a case or locating fresh research topics, in order to empower attorneys.

Case Study:

- AI-Powered Financial Advisors: AI-powered financial advising tools can offer insights into investing plans, but their true worth lies in giving customers concrete actions based on their own objectives. AI might, for instance, provide a roadmap for portfolio diversification depending on the user's financial objectives and risk tolerance in addition to explaining why a specific investment is a wise decision.

We can turn AI from a passive tool into a potent force for good by developing AI systems that are capable of more than merely explaining decisions and making sure that users can act on those explanations.

10.4 Fostering an Explainability Culture

It is crucial to institutionalize explainability in AI development and policy in order to guarantee that explainable AI becomes the norm across industries. Explainability must become a fundamental element of AI development, implementation, and assessment, necessitating a cultural change in businesses, governments, and regulatory agencies.

Putting Explainability Into Practice in AI Development

Explainability ought to be a crucial component of any organization's AI development approach. In order to create transparent, interpretable AI systems, it is necessary to establish clear guidelines and best practices. Additionally, it entails creating platforms and tools that make explainability easier so AI developers may incorporate explainable models into their systems with ease.

- Frameworks for Explainability in Governance: Organizations may maintain accountability and transparency by putting in place governance frameworks that give explainability top priority at every stage of the AI lifecycle, from design and development to deployment and monitoring. These guidelines ought to promote routine audits of AI systems to make sure they are operating as planned and provide clear justifications.

- The future of artificial intelligence is greatly influenced by governments and regulatory agencies. Regulators can aid in ensuring that AI technologies are developed responsibly by creating policies that require the usage of explainable AI and set requirements for transparency. Establishing XAI standards in partnership with leading industry players will promote innovation and trust across industries.

Establishing an Accountability Culture

Lastly, it's critical to establish a culture of accountability. Explainability must be given top priority by leaders in their companies, inspiring teams to develop AI systems that are not just efficient but also morally and transparently sound. Businesses may foster a sense of accountability among their AI teams and guarantee that the development and implementation of AI systems always take society's needs into account by establishing explainability as a fundamental value.

There are many obstacles in the way of creating ethical AI ecosystems, but there are also a ton of amazing potential. We can develop AI systems that are not only strong but also accountable, moral, and consistent with societal values by integrating explainability and ethics into education, showcasing real-world success stories, enabling users to act on AI insights, and encouraging an explainability culture within businesses. Although the path to responsible AI is not yet complete, it is attainable with cooperation and a concentrated effort.

ABOUT THE AUTHOR

 Author and thought leader in the IT field Taylor Royce is well known. He has a two-decade career and is an expert at tech trend analysis and forecasting, which enables a wide audience to understand complicated concepts.

Royce's considerable involvement in the IT industry stemmed from his passion with technology, which he developed during his computer science studies. He has extensive knowledge of the industry because of his experience in both software development and strategic consulting.

Known for his research and lucidity, he has written multiple best-selling books and contributed to esteemed tech periodicals. Translations of Royce's books throughout the world demonstrate his impact.

Royce is a well-known authority on emerging technologies and their effects on society, frequently requested as a speaker at international conferences and as a guest on tech podcasts. He promotes the development of ethical technology, emphasizing problems like data privacy and the digital divide.

In addition, with a focus on sustainable industry growth, Royce mentors upcoming tech experts and supports IT education projects. Taylor Royce is well known for his ability to combine analytical thinking with technical know-how. He sees a time when technology will ethically benefit humanity.